Table of Contents

Introduction
Why on earth would I setup an offshore team?
Reasons, Risks, and Rewards
Remote Project Management Can be Successful ... 17
The Pitfalls of Human Behavior and Managing Distributed Teams ... 22
Use Your Remote Teams Right - Industry Secrets From an Insider ... 29
The Art of Managing Remote Teams ... 37

Introduction

By: Hugo Messer

Eight years ago, I had set myself a goal: To master the art of managing remote teams. I started out serving web and software companies in the Netherlands on a fixed price model. We would try to get clear requirements and send them to our partners in Ukraine. They would estimate the project, provide a planning, and off we went. I figured out that this *'black box'* approach did not make anyone happy – neither our clients nor us. What did seem to work though was enabling our customers to work directly with our partner's developers. They would hire the programmer for a longer term and manage the programmer directly on a day-to-day basis. In the beginning, I thought I had the perfect model: link the programmer to the customer and off we went to the next customer. I was surprised that after a couple of months, I regularly got calls from clients who wanted to cancel the contract immediately. So, that did not work perfectly. A wise person once told me, "Hugo, it is better to join an established company to learn how and what they do, before starting your own." Maybe I should have listened...

The next step in finding a formula that worked was setting up our own offices with our own people. Thereupon we had more influence on who we hired, the culture inside the company, and how everybody worked. I strongly believe that the core values and the culture within a company have a big influence on how people behave. Furthermore, we made the decision to become excellent at the *'dedicated model'* in which customers have their own team members, managed directly by themselves. By focusing vigorously on this single delivery model, we learned what was needed and developed a model in which client, developer, and Bridge were satisfied.

After years of trial and error, I can say that managing remote teams is really an art. I had committed to learn how to do this and (still) spend days and nights figuring out what works best. For software company whose main business is to deliver software projects or products for another company working with developers, it seems even harder. The focus is on their core business and not on managing remote teams. Nevertheless one has to learn how to do it.

In this eBook, we want to share what I and others in the field of offshoring have learned. Maybe you're thinking about setting up an offshore team within your own company by collaborating with a partner or using freelancers. This eBook will give you insights into the reasons why people choose to set up an offshore team, the pitfalls they have walked into, and the things they did to avoid stepping into the same pitfalls again.

There is no clear path to success. Offshoring is all about people and, human behavior is unpredictable. Besides, the variables are different in each company's situation. It is more like juggling eight balls in the air than following a paved path. But there are certain areas that you can focus on in order to increase success. There are habits that create more positive results if your people build them in the right way. This eBook provides you with insights into the habits and focus areas that will help you succeed.

About this eBook

The main focus of the eBook is how not to screw up when managing a remote team. To answer this question, the first chapter zooms into why you would set up an offshore team. Your sole motive might be pure cost savings or to speed up your project in the short term. If those are the only motives, chances are big that you will be disappointed. Managing remote teams, with big geographical, cultural, and language gaps is not easy and needs careful thought and preparation.

Hugo Messer, a global staffing expert from the Netherlands, writes about the why from the *vendor's perspective*. Hugo has gained substantial experience in setting up and managing remote teams with suppliers, freelancers, and own offices.

Then **Zhenya Rozinskiy**, an experienced outsourcer from the US, writes from the *buyer's perspective* about the reasons, risks, and rewards. Zhenya has, for over 15 years, been involved in setting up remote development teams for companies of various sizes and in many different countries.

Furthermore, to prepare you for the journey, three authors share their insights into the pitfalls of offshoring and how to prevent them. They describe real practical lessons learned, supported by cases from their daily work. Each of them looks at success from a different angle, one as the liaison between the Netherlands and India, one as a consultant, and one as a nearshore provider.

Erik Joustra works for Tech Mahindra, a large Indian outsourcing company. He runs their Dutch office and acts as a delivery manager to accommodate Dutch multinationals working with their Indian teams. **Katie Gove** is the CEO of Trellis, a consulting company from Denmark focused on outsourcing. She has seen many projects go wrong and will share some of these stories as well as how to prevent them. **Nataly** lives in Ukraine and works for Intercomputer, an outsourcing provider from Ukraine. She has gained experience in different outsourcing companies in the past 10 years and looks at the pitfalls and success factors from the supplier's point of view.

This is the first eBook in a series of eBooks that will be published within a couple of months' interval and later on into one printed book. These eBooks are being written through a crowdwriting project and the authors are experts from all over the world.

We welcome any suggestions or feedback for further improvement. If you are interested in the upcoming eBooks or are an experienced practitioner who would like to contribute with your knowledge, please send an e-mail to h.messer@bridge-outsourcing.nl.

Why on earth would I setup an offshore team?

By: Hugo Messer

Before you embark on a successful offshoring 'trip', the first and most fundamental question to ask is, "Why would I do it?" Often, the first reason that pops into the mind is 'to save costs'. Media is always talking about 'moving work to low wage countries'. Projects that are reported in newspapers are those of big companies cutting thousands of jobs in their home countries while replacing them with people from India. Without denying that companies can realize cost savings (and this is certainly interesting for any company), let us look into a few other reasons and benefits.

In my view, the best reason to offshore is 'value creation by attracting talented people'. If the focus is on creating extra value for customers (through better innovation, faster time to market, higher quality, etc.), the success of offshoring is then seen from another perspective than with a focus on mere cost savings. If your measurement is based on how much cost you have saved, then you evaluate everything that happens using these 'glasses'. If on the other hand, you focus on creating extra value, you may measure the number of ideas that have come from your offshore team or the extra features that have been added to your software product. Through such glasses, success gets another definition – a definition that is more likely to bring real benefits to your customers.

Looking only at the costs, you may conclude after 6-12 months that your savings goal has not been reached. You may ignore all the other achievements the offshoring project has realized and/or the time frame you are looking at may not be long enough. As with most projects in the world, it sometimes takes longer and is probably more expensive than you expected. This causes people to conclude that the project was unsuccessful, even though the result, i.e. the value, might actually be positive.

To create a solid foundation for making your offshoring project a success, you need to think carefully about the motives of starting the project. Below is an overview of the primary benefits companies can achieve through offshoring.

1. Attract Talent

The first and foremost reason to engage in offshoring, in my opinion, is to attract talent. Your company strives to create massive value for customers, and for this, you need the smartest brains in the world. Engaging bright and creative people to tackle your problems will boost innovation in your organization, thus raising the delivered value.

One of the biggest challenges for (software) companies today is finding the right programmers. In Europe as well as in the US, there is a huge shortage of engineers. Companies are looking to hire the brightest engineers. In the years to come, this shortage will increase because the population will grow old and very few people get a technical degree. This means that if you stay focused on the local labor market, you will be fishing in the same pond as everyone else, including your competitors.

By attracting talent from offshore or nearshore, you enable your company to involve these bright people much more easily. The labor pool you are tapping into is substantially larger and there are motivated people that would love to start working for you straightaway. To understand the scale at which this is (and will be) happening, you can read the research which Hackett Group recently published about the future of offshoring. The research was carried out among 4700 companies with a turnover of USD 1 billion or more. The researchers predict that by 2016, 2.3 million jobs would have been moved offshore from the US and Europe. This represents 1/3 of total jobs in IT, finance, procurement, and HR. Out of these, 40% will go to India.

At the same time, the EU will have a shortage of over 700,000 people in IT by 2015 and 90% of all jobs will include an IT component. The IT sector is growing rapidly as companies become dependent on IT systems for operations and growth. Hence, companies have a big incentive to move jobs offshore or nearshore.

By 2030, Europe will be staring at a stagnant population with twice as many citizens older than 65 than children under 15. In the US, this figure is quite different; by 2030, there will be 65 million more Americans, with children outnumbering the seniors.

The US is also open to immigrants. As Fareed Zakara puts it: "Without immigration, U.S. GDP growth over the last quarter century would have been the same as Europe's. America's edge in innovation is overwhelmingly a product of immigration. Foreign students and immigrants account for 50 percent of the science researchers in the country. In 2010, foreign students get more than 50 percent of all PhDs awarded in every subject in the US." At the same time, the US is embracing offshoring. They pioneered offshoring and they still dominate the industry, sending much more work offshore than Europe.

The US has one main objective: grow and stay competitive in a globalized world. Europeans tend to think in another way. Some governments are coming to power on the promise of limiting immigration. The US government motivates immigrants to come there to work, whereas the EU tends to close its borders and make it hard for people to join the European countries, even if they are knowledgeable migrants. When foreign workers from Eastern Europe come to our countries to work in construction and similar fields, people wonder 'why are they taking our jobs at much lower rates?' And offshoring is still in its infancy!

For Europe, the main way to remain competitive and to keep on growing in the decades to come is to embrace offshoring on a big scale. Our population is aging; there is no doubt about that. We do not like to invite large groups of foreigners to our country (as has been done in the 50s when Northern Africans joined our labor forces to fill the gaps). So, if we do not have enough local people, if we do not want to bring people to the jobs, then we should take the jobs to other people in other countries.

To put things in perspective, it is also interesting to look at the number of engineering graduates in different countries. Sweden adds about 3,000 new technology graduates every year, while the Netherlands adds about 7,000. In India, close to 3 million people graduate each year, of which 16% graduate in the fields of science and technology. Ukraine has 610,000 yearly graduates of which 24% are in the fields of science and technology.

I regularly read about this topic in Netherland's media and the striking thought is some people's claim that there is actually no shortage of technically skilled talent. While the industry and government, for instance, claim a shortage of about 8,000 – 15,000 programmers, others point to the many programmers who've been laid off and are sitting idle at home (usually the older people). My view on this is that something is wrong; there is a clear mismatch in the labor market. Even if the numbers for a whole country or continent may differ from reality, in a specific city for a specific company, the shortage can clearly exist.

2. Create a Flexible Workforce and Cost Structure

In most European countries, labor laws are very strict. Once you hire someone and that person works for you for a year or more, it becomes hard or costly to let the person go. These laws were invented decades ago to protect workers and provide long term employment. In today's turbulent economic times, an inflexible workforce is a burden to companies, especially to smaller, agile businesses. Nobody knows what people and how many one will need tomorrow.

Most companies think in terms of 'employees in the office', because this is the way of organizing we are used to. If it becomes hard to find the right person to work in your office, you may engage freelancers, employment agencies, or external suppliers. This has the advantage of having local people that can work in your office and the contracts are flexible. The disadvantage: it is expensive. Besides, the search is local and even the external companies search in the same labor pool, thus the risks are that it will not easily bring the right person to the right position.

Companies benefit from offshoring because they can easily scale up when needed. If a large project is started, a team of developers can be added to the existing team. Once this project is over, the contract can be terminated and the people will be moved to another customer's project (if the setup is not a captive center but a partner). If things get rough and you have a hard time keeping your local people at work, you can easily remove some team members or stop them altogether. These decisions are harder and costlier when working with local employees. With flexible termination dates, it becomes easier to increase or decrease labor costs as the economic situation demands.

An example of a project that I had recently managed is an incubator from Switzerland. During the summer of 2012, they got funded and they acquired a dating platform from a big publisher in Germany. They laid out a roadmap for further development of the dating platform and started with a team of three Java developers in our Kiev operation. In the fall of 2013, they added two more developers to speed up. From August 2012 till June 2013, the team developed features cooperating with a scrum master located in the customer's Zurich office. By May 2013, it became clear to the CEO that their funds were running out and they decided to stop the development until they got a new round of funding. If the startup would have worked with local employees, they would not have gained the same speed as it would have been much harder and costlier to hire five developers in Switzerland. This is especially a concern for startups as the future is uncertain; nobody knows how long the startup will run and people are reluctant to join them. A CEO will also be more reluctant to hire a large team, knowing he or she might have to fire them a few months later. However, by using the remote setup, they were able to achieve their goals.

At what point in time do you consider hiring offshore talent? I discussed this question with one of our customers in an outdoor swimming pool under the Cochin sun, because he was visiting his offshore team (a nice side effect of offshoring). They have developed a software product for managing digital assets using some non-mainstream technologies. In Germany, it was not possible for them to find the right people. They had searched for employees by running ads, searching in their network, and engaging recruiters. They had searched for freelancers and external suppliers. But no solution brought enough people to further develop their product fast enough. Since they had an employee with ties to Serbia, they started a pilot with two Serbian freelancers. This brought the awareness about offshoring as an option. With us, they created a team of 9 people, personally hand picked and managed on a day-to-day basis by their own managers.

Many companies do not consider offshoring at all or consider it at a later stage. This might have to do with the perceived complexity and the changes that have to be made in the organization. It might also relate to the perception of 'outsourcing', where you describe a desired outcome in a requirements document, send that to a supplier and let them execute it. If outsourcing is perceived as 'hiring talent', either through setting up your own company offshore or by engaging with an offshore staffing supplier, many companies might solve their talent problem with ease.

3. Save Costs

This is what everybody strives for and many times it is the primary reason to engage in offshoring. As described earlier, it is also the reason why so many people consider their offshoring project a failure too early. The big questions with saving costs through offshoring are how soon can you expect the cost savings and how much do you want to save. The undeniable fact is that in the startup period, you have the highest costs and over time they go down. But most companies do not have the stamina to go through this startup period if they conclude that they did not save enough.

The initial period has some activities that will raise the costs. Firstly, management needs to figure out how to set up the team, if they should do it on their own or with a partner, what country to choose, etc. Then, the team has to be selected, the project has to be specified, and the team needs to think about the way they will cooperate and communicate. Next, (this is the most unexpected cost for many companies) your project manager will spend way more time than you wished in the initial months of setting up the collaboration. This person is probably new to this way of working, new to the offshore team members, and has to find a balance in collaborating with the local team and the offshore team. He must figure out the skills of each remote team member, how to communicate best with everyone, how much specification each person needs for their work, etc.

There will be communication problems and the teams have to communicate on how to overcome these. The project manager needs to learn many things and it takes time. If you assume that you will simply add some remote team members and your project manager can go on as he or she has always done, you will be deceived. Another certainty is that over time, this gets better especially if the offshore team grows; the time spent will be relatively less per person and productivity goes up.

Another aspect related to costs is the question about where you choose to be located. There are big differences in salaries between the bigger IT hubs and the smaller towns. Bridge has one office in Kiev, where salaries are 25-50% higher than in our office in Odessa. The Indian office we have is in Cochin, where salary costs are less than half of what they are in Bangalore and Mumbai. Even though Mumbai is among the least expensive cities in the world regarding the cost of living, it is among the top most expensive cities to buy property, according to the Global Property Guide. Property in Kiev is also very expensive. Hence the choice of location does impact how much you can save.

The model you choose also affects the cost level. Setting up your own offshore company may seem to be the cheapest option. From my experience, I have learned that you always substantially underestimate the investment and costs of such a venture. The operational costs could be low once it runs smooth, but to get there, the investment is so large (taking into account the research, the trips, the legal formalities, finding the right team, making mistakes, etc.) that eventually it will bring lower costs only if you consider this over a longer period of time. The big multinationals started out by setting up their own offices in India and most of them sold the companies to local suppliers later on to become their customers.

Working with a partner also has many flavors. The fundamental choice is whether to engage a local company with an offshore setup that can service you (which adds to the cost since the company has overhead in your country) or to find a supplier directly in the country you choose. In both cases, the price range will be large.

Lastly, I experience varying ways of calculating the cost savings. In our case, companies hire a dedicated team in one of our development offices. They incur the benefits of having a flexible external workforce and yet they frequently compare the costs with having employees in their company. By doing that, they often consider only the gross salary, not the other costs. While I realize that all of my clients might do this for negotiation purposes, I believe that the real comparison should be between hiring a local freelancer or staffing company and the offshore setup. It should then include all costs such as social security, holidays, travel expenses, phone, desk, workplace, etc. These costs are usually included in the rate of an offshore vendor. Furthermore, it is fair to add to the comparison, a percentage of your local project manager's time. By making the right calculation, you might get a more favorable case for cost savings.

4. Launch Products Faster

Many companies try to launch their products using their current team. Some people might be added gradually but as their business is launching products, they usually cannot be the best at scouting for talent continually. By learning how to work with remote teams, you can add team members according to the launch schedule you lay out. You can scale up with another team if you want to launch faster or scale down if you anticipate a delay. Since costs are typically lower for remote team members, you can add more people to your team with the same budget.

If you set up a smooth remote collaboration, you could even go so far as to have a full product team offshore, including the product owner. Your local team can focus on the core products and you can engage the offshore team in launching new products. Another alternative is that your local team implements customizations for customers, while the offshore team develops new generic features. Both these approaches will bring higher speed to your company.

5. Gain Access to Local Markets

This is often not the primary reason for setting up a remote team and it is also often overlooked. The markets in Europe and the US are stagnating or growing slowly, while developing countries like India are growing much faster. For instance, today there are 125 million Indians with access to the Internet, which represents 10% of the population. In the next decade, this number is likely to double or even triple. The developing countries will experience over a billion people moving into the middle class in the next decade. These are all potential buyers of your product or service. If you have a successful business that could be replicated in another country, it is surely worth exploring. It is a small step to hire a few marketing or sales people in your remote team once you have a development team in place. Alternatively, your supplier may partner with you to launch your product in their country.

6. Change the World and Have Fun

Last but not least is a personal reason to run a global IT staffing company. In the world of business, many people consider costs and rational reasons and may laugh at 'having fun' as a reason for embarking on any business venture. However, my logic is this: We all go on holidays; most of us enjoy exploring other cultures and meeting people that are different from us. I personally love talking to my Indian, Ukrainian, Swedish, Swiss, and German colleagues every day. I find it inspiring to have the whole world on the screen of my PC. I love learning how to overcome cultural differences and challenges in communication. By learning this, I am able to help others do the same.

Meanwhile, I get to travel regularly to our offices, which I enjoy most of the time. I also believe that this is the future; crowdsourcing, offshoring, nearshoring, open source projects, and companies encouraging their employees to work from home. It all boils down to people collaborating through the Internet from any place in the world. The world becomes a global village and people get more used to collaborating remotely. We will need to do this because it is hard to find talent locally and our competitors are engaging offshore talent and will outdo us if we do not. So why not be the first?

About Hugo Messer

Hugo Messer

Hugo Messer has been building and managing teams around the world for over 7 years. His passion is to enable people that are spread across cultures, geographies, and time zones to collaborate. Whether it's offshoring or nearshoring, he knows what it takes to make a global collaboration work.

To know more about Hugo, check out his website http://www.hugomesser.com. You can also read blogs at http://www.bridge-outsourcing.com or watch videos at http://www.youtube.com/user/BridgeBroadcasting/.

About Bridge Global IT Staffing

Bridge Global IT Staffing offers western software companies an opportunity to work with IT talents from their offices in India and Ukraine. The personal support, offered from the European offices in the Netherlands, Germany, Switzerland, Sweden, and Denmark, makes it easier for clients to manage their colleagues from a distance. Since there is both an offshore and a nearshore office, chances are high that Bridge has the talented IT employee you are looking for. If not, the perfect candidate will be found for you. Website: http://www.bridge-outsourcing.nl

Reasons, Risks, and Rewards

By: Zhenya Rozinskiy

So you have made the decision to outsource. Maybe you have even selected a provider and finalized your plans. You are now ready to get started. You think you have figured it out. Your provider is telling you that they will manage everything. You will be getting regular updates and they will take care of all your problems. After all, that is what they do. They have done it for many other clients and will do it for you too. You are their most important client because they want more business, they want your name on their portfolio, and they need to impress you.

Is that you? If so, you are in for a world of surprises.

The harsh reality is that no one but you will make this project a success. After all, your provider employs people, and by nature, people are not perfect.

In this collection of eBooks, a group of outsourcing specialists will share their experiences of starting and managing an outsourcing project and provide some ideas to get you started. We all come from different backgrounds, ranging from being customers to running outsourcing companies. What unites us is the passion for making outsourcing successful. We believe that with the right approach and proper structure, having an outsourcing team can be the best decision you make for your company and for yourself. We also believe that saving money is not the primary reason to outsource. It's a great side effect but one that you will only achieve if you take the proper steps in managing your outsourcing endeavors.

People turn to outsourcing for different reasons. In some cases, their executive team has made the decision and told them, "Go, execute." In others, it is out of necessity to either cut costs or produce more results while maintaining costs. It could also be because you have a short-term project and it's just easier to have someone else do it. Regardless of why you got here, you are charged with making it work. If you were not, you would not be reading this eBook, now would you?

During my first outsourcing project, I learned that outsourcing is a risk. I got involved in outsourcing over 15 years ago. It was right on the peak of the DOT COM boom. Money grew on trees, but finding good people to execute our projects was hard. In fact, it was so hard that we had to plan projects around when we could hire developers to build them. There were points where we had to skip customer requests because we simply did not have the people to do the work.

It was during this period that I was approached by the CEO of the company I worked for, who suggested that we try this new thing: offshoring. I fought it at first. After all, I was afraid; I was outsourcing my own job. Nevertheless, I started looking for a provider, and I came across a company that promised me the world. Their rates were less than one fourth of what we paid locally, and that included the rate for the people that would actually be doing the work: project managers, local oversight, etc. I thought it was the perfect setup. Alas, as you can probably guess, that project was a miserable failure for the company. It was, however, a tremendous success for me – I learned some hard lessons but I realized that outsourcing can work only if done right.

As with anything in life, your outsourcing projects come with risks and rewards. And, as it frequently happens, the higher the risk, the higher the reward. Before you start, you have to weigh both sides to find the best strategy for your company to reap the most rewards. And we are here to help. Below, you will find the top reasons, risks, and rewards that I have discovered as a consumer and a consultant of outsourcing engagements.

Top Reasons

Talent

The main reason one should get into outsourcing is for the talent. The world is full of wonderful, smart, and hardworking people. They are well educated, experienced, and eager to help you achieve your goals. Not every company can have their headquarters in Silicon Valley or fly a specialist in to work on a project. Outsourcing can introduce you to people from all across the world that have the talent to complete your project.

Smaller companies and companies that are not geographically located near the people who have the skills to assist them, can get their projects completed through outsourcing. You do not have to reinvent the wheel and hire a full-time person, or build a department. If a vendor has the knowledge, skills, and technique to complete your project and meet or exceed your expectations, you should choose them. Outsourcing allows you a wider pool of candidates to choose from so you can get the best for your company.

Availability of a Skill Set

Do you have a portion of your system that is a little outdated or do you use a technology that is not popular in your area? Is it hard to find people to update your systems? If you answered yes, then outsourcing is a viable solution. It allows you to tap into a worldwide pool of resources and find the best people to get the job done.

You cannot be a jack of all trades. Even if you were to keep the project completely in-house, you are not going to be able to do every part of the project. Whether it is lack of knowledge in the particular area or just lack of time, outsourcing can lift that burden off your shoulders. You can contract individuals or a company that is knowledgeable in a skill set and let them focus on that aspect of your project. In turn, by using external resources you will be able to build your core competency around the backbone of your operation.

Focus

Do you have an area that is necessary to support your product, but it is not the focus of your company? Secondary projects and smaller tasks are great to outsource because they let you focus on your company's larger goals. If the core of your company is software development you can outsource your website maintenance and get back to designing the new update.

When the project is completely in-house, it is easy to overlook those secondary areas. They are back burner projects and you may never give them the attention they need. Through outsourcing, those projects will be as important as your core area and will get as much dedication as anything else you are working on and paying for.

Flexibility

Do you have a temporary surge of work? Maybe you are releasing a new version of your software or have a new client that requires some customization. Using outsourcing for this type of project is almost always a perfect solution. You will only pay for the time people actually work on your project and it will free up your internal staff to focus on larger assignments.

Outsourcing can also provide you with flexibility in time management. If there is a tight deadline for a project, you can outsource it to a vendor in a different time zone so that the work can still be done even if your office is closed. There are also many companies that have an in-house team working on the project during business hours and then an outsourced team working on it through the night. That way, you can be assured that your project is being worked on the entire day and it will get completed sooner.

Budget Friendly

Sometimes, you have the possibility to move some of your budget from full-time employees to contractors. It could just be the way your budgets are set up or because you do not want to demonstrate long term liabilities for your firm. Whatever the reason might be, using a third party is a good way to shift your spending.

Staying within budget is on par with providing an excellent product. Your customers will be happy and you can be secure in the knowledge that your company is not in financial trouble because of the project. If you are near the limit of your budget, you can reduce your expenses by outsourcing and shift the money so you have more leeway to complete the project.

Reduce Costs

Hiring a full-time, in-house employee comes with a lot of overhead costs. You have to worry about vacation/sick time, health insurance, and worker's compensation, on top of the costs to stock their space with supplies and the electronics they need so they can actually do their job. And then, there is the salary.

Not every company has to worry about all of these costs but outsourcing can significantly reduce your expenditure. You still have to pay your vendor, but in most cases, you do not have to worry about any of the added costs. You do not have to buy their computer and worry about maintaining it and you are not paying their taxes. Many vendors are independent contractors so the liability is on them, and even if you go through an outsourcing company, that company is incurring those costs.

Top Risks

Low Employee Morale

Any time you mention the word 'outsourcing', people begin to wonder if their job is safe. This is especially true if you have recently gone through layoffs or lost a big client. There is no way around it, and you will need to face it sooner or later. Being transparent and clearly communicating your intentions with your employees will help minimize this risk.

It can be very easy to ignore this reaction to outsourcing, especially if it does not show up immediately. However, you must have a plan in place to combat low employee morale, regardless of when you decide to tackle the issue. Assure your employees that they are valued and the outsourcing endeavor will be used to free up their time to focus on other tasks.

Reduced Productivity

At the outset of an outsourcing endeavor, you will experience initial loss of productivity. Regardless of what your provider may promise you, it will happen. Imagine if you replaced your entire local team today with a new group. Even if your new hires are the best in the business they will still need time to learn your systems, your company, and come up to speed. The same happens when you bring in a new remote team.

There are additional challenges with training a remote team since they are not in the same office to be trained face to face. Expect to spend the first few weeks building on your contacts and answering a lot of questions from the vendor. Make sure that you plan for the learning curve and have someone available to help your vendor get stable in their role as a part of your company. To avoid a large impact on your services, you can always plan to implement an outsourcing project during a slow period in your business.

Burnout

If you are not careful, you might burn out some people on both sides of your partnership. Depending on your vendor, challenges can arise because you may be working across multiple time zones, with cultural differences, and possibly even a language barrier. Burnout can happen at any point in time, whether it is during the implementation stage or once the project is complete.

It is wise to regularly reassess the number of tasks and their deadlines to ensure that your vendor is not being overburdened. Conversely, you need to keep your in-house employees in mind as well. Outsourcing requires a coordinated effort from both parties and there should be at least one point of contact in your home office. If your project spans multiple departments, consider having multiple points of contact that span the departments so no one person is overloaded.

Loss of Knowledge

Outsourcing can be a short-term or long-term endeavor and in both cases, you are giving up some control to the vendor. If you give up too much control and let your vendor design and maintain your systems, you may face a situation where the vendor is the only one that knows how it works. It then becomes difficult to change vendors or even bring it back in-house. Your company will have to learn or relearn the system before you can move forward.

Regardless of the scope of your project, think carefully about what areas you want to outsource and ensure that someone in-house has the ability to manage it when there is a need. Otherwise that downtime, while you relearn your system, can disrupt services to your clients and hurt your company in the long run.

Bad Partnerships

Just like friendships and relationships between people, an outsourcing partnership may not work out. Not establishing clear and measurable goals may lead to a situation where you are still under a contract but not getting what you need. Communication is crucial to having a good partnership but even that is not foolproof. A vendor can embellish their skills to get your business; you need to be diligent and supervise the project.

It comes down to this: If you believe that the people on the other side are not as smart or as capable as your local employees, why bother outsourcing? After all, they will be developing a product that you will put your name on. You will have to communicate with them either directly or through a provider. Do you really want to work with someone you do not respect?

Top Rewards

Save Money

Cutting costs should not be the primary reason to outsource, but it is a great reward for the hard work you are doing. With many vendors, you pay much less for a similarly qualified employee than you would locally. There is no shame in it. Despite what you might read and hear about low wages paid by western companies when they offshore to different countries, it is all relative. It might sound very low by US or European standards, but it can be a very highly paid position in your provider's country.

It all comes down to the cost of living. If you choose to use a vendor in another country, in most cases, their cost of living is drastically lower than the United States. The average rent for an apartment is seven times higher in Silicon Valley than it is in Bangalore, India. Utilities cost six times more in San Jose than in Bangalore and food prices are nearly triple.

Outsourcing to India, or to another country with a lower cost of living, translates into cost savings for you.

Improved Productivity and Job Satisfaction for Local Employees

In every position, there is serious work that needs to be done. Whether it is fielding customer suggestions or electronically filing paperwork, these tasks are necessary but they take time away from your employees focusing on the company's goals. Using an offshore workforce will provide an avenue to export all the 'need to be done' tasks while allowing your local employees to focus on new and exciting projects.

Time after time, research shows that employee satisfaction comes first from the work they are doing. If you keep your employees challenged and allow them to do what they enjoy they will be more productive and happier. Outsourcing can take all the 'boring' but necessary tasks out of the equation so your employees will be excited when they come to work.

Freedom to Scale

Using an external vendor offers great flexibility in how your relationship is structured. The traditional 9 – 5 job is completely changed through outsourcing. It allows you to arrange your timeline around what needs to be completed. If your project has certain tasks that need to be done at different times of the day and night, you can outsource that to a vendor who will be awake and be able to complete the tasks.

Outsourcing also opens up possibilities of having a pool of candidates to choose from. Do you need a vendor only to troubleshoot problems when you have a software update? You most likely are not coming out with an update every week; so in this case, you can outsource to someone on a floating basis. You send them the work when you have it and you do not have to worry about keeping someone in a full-time position.

Travel

Who said you cannot have some fun while working? While being engaged in my outsourcing activities I have traveled to many countries, visited many cities, and met countless scores of great people. Many of them have become my friends for life.

Yes, outsourcing has its perks. It requires personal interactions and that means getting on a plane and traveling. How about seeing Taj Mahal or visiting the Great Wall of China while being dined and wined by your outsourcing providers? On the other hand, it also allows you the freedom to take vacations while knowing your project is in safe hands. When you have a long-term productive relationship with a vendor, you can take that trip you have been putting off because the project has stabilized.

Outsourcing is not about cutting corners on price or design; it is about creating a great product that your company would be glad to call its own. These are the many advantages of outsourcing and there will always be specific risks depending on your project and field. It is up to you to research and apply them to your company and projects to create the best outsourcing experience possible.

As you continue reading, you will come across a variety of experiences and tips to help you understand the nuanced process of outsourcing and how to avoid common mistakes. Outsourcing is a process but you have taken the first step in the right direction.

About Zhenya Rozinskiy

Zhenya Rozinskiy has over 20 years of experience in the software development industry. During this time, Zhenya has had numerous opportunities to help grow and make many companies of different sizes and different maturity levels successful. His experience includes delivering shrink-wrapped software, enterprise solutions, custom product implementations, and high-availability, high-traffic eCommerce sites. After first getting into outsourcing and offshoring development models and failing, Zhenya made it his personal challenge to find a way to make outsourcing work. Now, 16 years later and after successfully launching offshoring teams in almost every continent, Zhenya has acquired a unique know-how for successful software development outsourcing. By combining his years of experience working with people and building effective teams with his practical approach to outsourcing, Zhenya has become a recognized thought leader in all areas of establishing and growing responsive engineering organizations.

Remote Project Management Can be Successful

By: Erik Joustra

In today's globalized world, technology and IT infrastructure have enabled alternative strategies such as outsourcing and offshore development. In this article, I'd like to discuss the hot topic of performing projects overseas. Is project management using an offshore team really very different from using a team located on another floor in your office building? Do you really need special (or different) skills to manage your project differently?

In my opinion, the difference is minimal when you consider the basic activities. Naturally, there are obvious differences such as language, culture, and physical or sometimes geographical distance. However, magnifying these differences can turn them into problems. If you believe that any of these problems is too big, you may use it as an excuse not to offshore the execution of a project. I believe this is not a legitimate excuse.

To be honest, in my early experiences, I too thought that these obvious differences would be a pain in the neck. However, eventually as my experiences increased, it seemed to be a matter of getting used to and learning how to deal with them. After all, other parts of the world also use Prince II, ITIL, and whatever other best practice standards you can name (that we in the western world may not always use to perfection). These are industry standards.

During my 15 years of experience in outsourcing, and especially using offshore and nearshore execution of projects and maintenance services, I have learned far too many lessons. In the following paragraphs, I will highlight three of the most common problems that I have faced and learnt from.

No Black Box Approach

In the early days of offshoring, companies talked about a 'Black Box' approach. Phrases like *"I do not mind HOW they do it!"* and *"They will obviously know themselves..."* were quite common. To be honest, this mindset was not a surprise. Were we not doing this internally too? Throwing things over the wall and being surprised when we received the first deliverable? The first time we assigned something to India, we were fully surprised when the first deliverable did not meet our expectations. We wondered, *"How could this be?"* Whereas we actually had the same experience internally before we did any outsourcing!

To avoid possible problems that the Black Box approach could cause, I believe that we should treat an offshore team the same way as we would like to treat an on-site team. So, what does this mean? For example, when we have a team on-site, we involve members of the team in interactions with the business or clients of the project. We organize sessions, workshops, newsletters, and everything else that is needed. We make sure they understand the business and what they need to produce.

Follow the same approach with your remote team. Visit them (with your end user) or let them visit you. In addition, today's technology of Video Conferencing can bridge the geographical distance. The aim is to make the team part of your total environment; simple things like pictures, logos, movies, etc. can help you in this. In one instance, we set up a complete video introduction of all the people on the team (on-site and offshore). The video was part of the Starter Kit that we handed out to every new member on the team. The Starter Kit also included a walk-through video of the process that needed to be supported by the new system. The walls of the team rooms in both Netherlands and India were filled with pictures and drawings of the Program. Everyone was invited to the monthly team session, no matter where in the world they were located. In another Program, we even set up a daily Skype Video Link between the two parts of the team.

The lesson is simple – treat your remote team as you would treat employees in your own office building.

No Two Captains on the Same Ship

I have always believed, during the first years of my experience, that project management can only be done when you are part of the team and cannot be performed out of an ivory tower (from a distance). But how do you go about this when part of your team works from a remote location? If we go by the above thesis, it will not work when you have a project manager onsite managing a remote team. The most obvious solution would then be to appoint two project managers – one onsite and one offshore, both at the same level. However, this will result in two captains on one ship, and we all know that this hardly works.

This leaves us with the question – is there a solution to this problem? When we look at the Indian culture we will soon realize that most professionals do have a keen sensitivity towards hierarchy. So we can use these cultural aspects in setting up the management of our remote team (combined with the on-site parts).

I have found out during the past years that when an offshore project manager reports to an onsite overall program manager (preferably from the end-user) it works much better than when the offshore project manager is kept at arms-length by putting a local project manager in between. A good example of this is the following case. Large offshore programs are mostly done by the large system integrators (SI). When we look at the Dutch market especially, the SIs have still a large pool of own personnel that one way or the other needs to be involved in the different programs. This 'legacy' problem is found within all companies.

In one of the examples, we examined a bad working program and because of that, a bad working relationship between a large Dutch customer and a large Dutch system integrator. The SI had offshored most of the development roles with a local project manager to manage a team of over 30 developers. The Dutch part of the team consisted of the functional design people and two project managers (one for the Design, and one for the Development). The program and steering meetings were in Dutch with the Dutch members where the on-site project manager represented the offshore team.

This lead to a lot of misunderstanding and misinterpretation, and a development team that was kept away at a distance. I will spare you the details, but as soon as the on-site development program manager was taken out of the governance, and replaced with the offshore project manager (directly reporting to the overall (customer) program manager), the communication drastically improved. The offshore project manager got more status, as he now directly reported to the program manager. He felt more responsible and had the opportunity to directly discuss issues with the program management team. The result was a much better performing development team, ending in a much better accepted end product, and based on a much better relationship.

So, do not have two captains on one ship, and know that offshore project managers know very well what they are talking about (maybe even better than our local colleagues).

Bridge the Cultural Gap

When starting an offshore/nearshore collaboration, no doubt you will experience cultural differences. I believe that to meet these differences in the best possible way, it is important to participate in workshops about the culture you are working with. Certainly, it is not sufficient to have knowledge of the culture of the offshore company (in this example, India); the cultural exchange must go both ways. Therefore, a workshop on the Dutch culture is a necessity too. The Indian colleagues will need to know how we behave as well as how we need to be aware of their behavior. We need to know details about each other such as what is important in the business culture, how things are being handled, and more specifically, how the culture within the company is? You can imagine that there will be differences which you need to address in both teams together.

To provide an example, Dutch business people often have an opinion about everything and do not hesitate to speak up. In the Indian culture, people's opinions are usually communicated through the hierarchical route. This means that an Indian colleague could take your personal opinion as a company statement. I have experienced many of these misunderstandings in the past, sometimes leading to complete change in the direction of the project, whereas one person just found a podium for his opinion. There are many examples of similar cases. Make sure you do not plan the culture workshop only once, but keep repeating it during the time you are working together.

When people understand, accept, and respect different cultures, the collaboration will become much smoother. Also, elaborating on examples during the project (both good and bad), will help to understand each other better.

Culture workshops also introduce the element of fun. You will get to learn more about your own culture and discover strange habits. You will also find out many things that you share in common. For instance, I always say that most Dutch experience the loss of the national football team as a painful experience, but when we lose to Germany it becomes a national disaster. I found out that the Indians understand this as the same goes for them when their national cricket team loses to Pakistan.

Something else to be careful about is the English language. We must remember that English is a foreign language for everyone involved (also for Indians even though it is one of India's official languages). This can cause a huge misunderstanding when people are directly translating words from their mother tongue into English. It also means that all communication needs to be in English. We do have a tendency to communicate in our native language when nobody else is around. We make slides and write e-mails in Dutch and that is both common and understandable. However, when we want to reuse the presentation or forward the e- mail, we will have some trouble. Since the colleagues in the foreign country will not be able to understand, you will have to invest additional time in translating information. This may be obvious facts for some of us, but I have seen it so many times (and still come across it) that I believe it is worth mentioning it.

In this essay, I have tried to give some examples of how remote project management can be successful. The examples are from my personal experience and I have worked in all the places. Whenever I start new projects or advice on them, I am conscious of the factors mentioned here. Sometimes they seem obvious, but most times they are forgotten in the rush of the project. Spending time on this will pay back heavily during the course of the project and therefore also, in the end. So, do not forget to use your common sense...it pays off.

About Erik Joustra

Erik Joustra is a Senior Manager with broad experience in different fields of the ICT Landscape. Since 1988, he works in the industry and has been on 'both sides of the table'. The highlight of his career is building, restructuring, and fine tuning of different organizational departments and divisions around outsourcing. In the past, he has worked for CapGemini, Atos Origin, and Ordina, setting up units and divisions for executing large outsourcing projects and maintenance contracts. In between these roles, he was the CIO of Casema (from 2000 to 2003) where he set up a new IT Department in a fast-growing and changing market. After his time at Ordina, Erik advised several companies on issues around their outsourcing contracts, both for suppliers and customers. Currently, Erik Joustra works at the Indian company Tech Mahindra and is responsible for building the Dutch Delivery Centre of Tech Mahindra.

Tech Mahindra

Tech Mahindra is part of the USD 16.2 billion Mahindra Group and is a leading global systems integrator and business transformation consulting organization, focused primarily on the telecommunications industry. In 2013, the Mahindra Group received the Financial Times 'Boldness in Business' Award in the 'Emerging Markets' category. Their solutions portfolio includes Consulting, Application Development & Management, Network Services, Solution Integration, Product Engineering, Infrastructure Managed Services, Remote Infrastructure Management and BPO Services, and Consulting. With an array of service offerings for TSPs, TEMs, and ISVs, Tech Mahindra is a chosen transformation partner for several leading wireline, wireless, and broadband operators in Europe, Asia-Pacific, and North America. Tech Mahindra has a global footprint through operations in more than 31 countries with 17 sales offices and 15 delivery centers. Assessed at SEI CMMi Level 5, Tech Mahindra's track record for value delivery is supported by over 47,400 professionals who provide a unique blend of culture, domain expertise, and in-depth technology skill sets.

The Pitfalls of Human Behavior and Managing Distributed Offshore Teams

By: Katie Gove

From: Talented_Indian_Engineer@Large_Outsourcing_Vendor.India;
Date: Mon, May 13, 2013 at 11:14 AM;
Subject: Optimal working conditions
To:
Danish_Project_Manager@Large_for_Denmark_But_Small_For_India_Client.Denmark

Dear Mr. Jensen:

We would like to request that we be permitted to lower the blinds in the programming room. It would help us tremendously if we could reduce the glare and the resulting heat. We have been able to tolerate it for the past three months but the onset of the summer season has prompted us to request this change.

Please get back to us at your earliest convenience.

Sincerely,
Vijay Gupta

It was at this point that the Danish project manager, Erik Jensen, realized that the management, communication, and governance environments of his remote team in India were not properly aligned to achieve the desired results.

Erik had assumed that sending off the requirement specification to the dedicated team of eight programmers and one project manager was enough to not only kick-start but also to deliver a successful project. Coupled with several 'team-building' e-mails about the great work that they were 'doing together', Erik thought he had cracked the code on managing remote teams.

What he found out during the ensuing three months was that this was not the case.

His hands-off management style, so common in Denmark, had created a vacuum of direction and leadership. Instead of enabling a team, he had stymied and confused them with his minimal involvement and guidance. And while his lack of management presence said one thing to the Indian team, his frequent reference to the 'team being critically important to the current round of development' left them grasping for some proof of him manifesting this apparent truth. Having never explicitly clarified the governance structure of the engagement, it was difficult for those involved to understand who had which roles and who had decision-making responsibility for what, often resulting in small technical and organizational issues landing on Erik's desk. These issues had percolated up since the engagement began, but Erik had always thought of them as a natural part of working out the kinks. Not until this e-mail did Erik realize that this 'kink' was really a fundamental disconnect between the desired results and the conditions necessary for success.

Managing remote teams is an art that transcends traditional project management. It is not enough to just have world-class processes, well-documented procedures, and a transparent governance structure, although achieving this *trifecta* is a daunting one in itself. Delivering projects successfully, let alone developing sustainable value-producing remote teams, means acknowledging the human dimensions of inter-personal and inter-organizational interaction. This means accommodating the cultural context, the personal and organizational goals of the folks involved, developing a diplomatic and detailed way of communicating, and investing a lot of time.

Mastering the art of managing remote teams means truly mastering communication including cultural context and language realities, engaging with remote teams as peers, and being prepared to invest both time and money in developing human and inter-organizational relationships to support remote teams.

Confusing Direction and Instruction with Communication

One of the common stumbling blocks for companies managing remote teams is that instruction is sometimes confused or conflated with communication. Instruction is critical. Communication is critical. However, they are not the same.

Instruction means specifying and guiding development and outcomes. This includes making sure that documentation and specifications are in good order. This is frequently not the case, particularly with companies that are relatively new to working with remote teams. It is not uncommon to see over-specification and over-control in the early phases of using distant teams. This does not necessarily mean that the sponsoring company is good at specifications and process management, just that they pour it on. It is also common to see the opposite: a lack of specification and a desire to 'just do it'. This means typically expressing orders for a process or competence that is presumed to be a commodity. In any event, dialog is one-way. In both cases, the quality and in the latter case, the quantity, of specifications is wholly unsuited to the desired results.

Contributing to this situation is that the organizations typically underestimate the tacit knowledge advantages that their internal and co-located teams have built into the working environment. Team members have accumulated good experience including overcoming previous challenges. This institutional memory is a critical advantage for project teams and it typically compensates for sub-optimal documentation. The problem is that knowledge is not documentation. When the company attempts to send the specifications to a remote team with no tacit knowledge advantages, the outcomes are guaranteed to be less than what could be achieved by the internal co-located team. Once the deficiency is acknowledged, companies usually try to put focus on documentation but it is rare that this competency is prioritized properly. The reality is that good documentation requires great skills but companies rarely put great resources on this task.

Equally challenging is effective *communication*. Typical expectations for managing remote teams are that e-mail, Skype, and an occasional trip can for the most part hold the efforts together. However, many companies often find out that these tools are not always good substitutes for sitting face-to-face, working together on a product, and solving problems. In addition, sponsoring organizations sometimes find that the direct and informal communication style typical among Danish managers is not the most effective tool for communication with remote teams. Often, to be able to successfully manage remote teams, organizations undergo a communications learning curve through which they develop clearer and more formal communications procedures and reporting along with cultivating an ability to communicate effectively in more hierarchical cultures.

Not unsurprisingly, *culture* and cultural differences can be a significant challenge in communicating with and managing remote teams. Danish culture believes in direct communication and an expectation of entrepreneurial spirit at work. That is not necessarily the default setting beyond the Øresund region. In more hierarchical cultures, which in effect mean almost every country to which Denmark outsources, offshores, and develops remote teams in, it is a sign of respect to defer to the client/partner. Teams typically will not do anything without being formally told and therefore wait for direction, often via proper documentation, prior to taking the next steps. The sparring that Danes value in their own professional relationships is frequently absent from these relationships as this kind of challenging interaction can be interpreted as making someone 'lose face'. Often Danes interpret this behavior that originates in respect as a lack of ownership and commitment.

Another challenge often found in communicating with and managing remote teams is *language*. Many experience that the company contacts and the upper-level resources are able to communicate well enough in a common language, typically English. However, it is not uncommon to see a leveling off of English ability once one gets to the operational team members. This, combined with a more hierarchical structure frequently found in firms outside of Denmark, can inhibit true cooperation and working-together by the operational team members. Resources in the remote teams are often disinclined to talk directly to their peers or necessary contacts at the sponsoring company and, are more likely to go through formal channels for communication. While this may adhere to the strict contract conditions, it can bring a formal and stilted characteristic to many of these relationships. This can eventually diminish the potential of the relationships to deliver successfully and productively.

The Default Position is Parent-Child, not Peer-to-Peer

There are two broad trends regarding how sponsors approach their relationship with their remote teams. Primarily, there are transactional relationships where the sponsor dictates terms and conditions and where the dialog more or less, goes in one direction. This is not to say that these kinds of relationships are not amicable or productive, but merely that the relationship is one of parent to child. The other kind of relationship, of which there are fewer, can be described as peer-to-peer.

There can be vast differences in productivity, costs, innovation, and satisfaction between these two kinds of relationships with the peer-to-peer type relationships delivering higher marks in all those categories. However, this does not mean that every peer-to-peer relationship can and does deliver at high levels or that parent-child relationship cannot. There are trends and differences between these two categories of relationships that are worth noting; this should spur sponsors to act deliberately to choose and develop one of the models based on desired results.

Where peer-to-peer relationships exist, one of the companies in the relationship may have had some experience with outsourcing, offshoring, and remote teams. It is quite possible that some dimension of that experience has been deeply negative and forced some critical process, governance, or management changes. The process of recognizing non-performing activities and taking corrective action enhances the sponsoring company's mastery of managing remote teams, thereby improving their confidence and ability to adapt to change.

Peer-to-peer relationships are more likely to occur when a sponsor engages a remote team in order to bring in new competencies and/or technologies rather than to supplement already existing in-house resources. Companies seem to be reluctant to engage in peer-to-peer relationships if both parties operate in the same area. We call this the 'paradox of expertise'. By this, we mean that it is often hard for experts to work with others in an area that they themselves master. There is a tendency to want to dominate and decide. It is particularly hard to delegate and to accept others' ways of doing things. Besides, resources at the sponsoring organization often feel that their job is vulnerable, that they can, in theory, be replaced. Their understanding of their value to the company can be shaken.

One of the key indicators of a peer-to-peer relationship is focusing on objectives rather than deliverables. This means setting the bar high and asking the remote team to come up with a qualitative plan to reach it. Another key to improve peer-to-peer relationships is the constant attention and cultivation of individual relationships among the resources on both sides. Being able to participate and receive recognition for ability and performance from the sponsoring company both catalyzes the remote team to reach higher and forces the sponsor's team to engage.

Failing to Invest in Personal Relationships

The lion's share of organizational focus within outsourcing and offshoring is centered on negotiating and contracting. Organizations are not typically prioritizing personal relationships, let alone cultivating them, when developing remote teams. However, failing to do so is one of the biggest mistakes a company can make. It is not uncommon for sponsoring organizations to be surprised at the amount of time it takes to build and cultivate these relationships. Often companies engage in outsourcing with the expectation that they are just 'buying' something which means putting in an order and waiting for delivery; or that they are merely 'lifting and shifting' an existing internal process to an offshore location. They are not prepared for more interaction and investment of time.

Typical of this is a large manufacturing organization that sponsors several large remote teams and says that when they started building remote teams, they started by describing technical skills that they needed for the product development process. They acknowledge that they wanted purely technical ability with no person attached. It was messy and they felt a distraction. They acknowledged that their Danish developers would quit if they were treated the same way. Yet, this is how they initially approached their remote team. This resulted in a good chunk of their remote team feeling commoditized and disenfranchised.

In coming to grips with the situation and turning it around, the organization discovered the importance of engaging with the person behind the technical skill. They were able to deliver on their large project goals even if the process was more involved than they originally expected. As the team lead noted, "It is so much less objective and so much more subjective than I would have thought. It is so personal and chemistry is so important. It is almost more about the relationship than the technology."

How Should Companies and Teams Tackle the Challenges of Distributed Teams?

Among the companies that are successfully managing remote teams, there are several shared characteristics:

First, there are **key resources managing the relationships** between the remote team's organization and the sponsor. These resources have general business competencies as well as a good degree of mastery of the sponsor's technology. However, they are less frequently the technical masters themselves. What seems to be crucial is that they have enough technical knowledge to manage and broker the interactions but they do not themselves play the role of technical specialist.

Secondly, there is consistent **scheduled and ad-hoc contact** between teams on both sides. This is critical. There appears to be a direct correlation between success as well as satisfaction and this exposure. It is critical that this exposure happens at several (preferably many) different levels between the partners and that there is regularity to it. Take the example of a large Northern European bank that has daily video conference calls between the IT Director and the COO in India. Having regularly scheduled communication builds a shared sense of commitment as well as an expectation of how things can and should be processed. In the example of the large Northern European bank, the topics range from operational to strategic; the philosophy is "a collection of small stones can damn the river" so it is far better to iron out the small things.

It is important that this consistent high-level interaction is supplemented by regular, individual, and ad-hoc interaction among the teams and resources. This means using some social time together, going out for a beer, or perhaps watching football or cricket together. In instances where there are only regular group/team meetings, we do not see the strengths and successes that are achieved by those with both regular group/team meetings and robust ad-hoc social interaction. Getting to know each other is critical for developing trust. There needs to be a **foundation of trust** that allows the various leaders and team members to dare to say "no" as well as to be honest about expectations, deadlines, deliverables, and progress. Without this foundation, it is quite difficult to transcend the rigid organizational roles of client and delivery organizations.

Thirdly, all the success **stories are built upon previous failures**. No company just leaps into success. The learning curve is so universal that there is hardly any company that does not have a story about their struggles in this arena. The fact is that successful programs have been able to learn from their less-than-satisfying experiences.

Fourth, sponsoring companies **formalize how partnering occurs** and clarify its **connection to business strategy** so that others in the organization understand it. This means that governance is clearly defined with specific details on all relevant roles and responsibilities. It also means being extremely clear about the business goals of the team. This clarity provides critical context and even motivation to all those involved.

A final key to successfully managing remote teams is that **the remote team itself must have a sense of ownership** regarding its work for the sponsor. It is worth noting that the contract itself does not guarantee, let alone deliver this. Ownership is the human dimension of the interaction, which means that the people responsible for the delivery have personal and professional pride in what they are delivering; they have something at stake.

This implies that the remote team is considered to be a part of the development team. They are treated equally; they are integrated into project meetings; their voice carries weight; expectations are high and they meet those expectations. They are not just given tasks to execute but rather given areas of responsibility about which they have a fair degree of latitude in determining solutions. This does not necessarily mean that they do not have requirement specifications, although there are many instances where that is the remote team's responsibility. What it does mean is that they succeed or fail based on their own merits and that the surrounding team(s) must interact with them on a more or less equal footing.

What is clear is that organizations have just begun to scratch the surface of the benefits of leveraging remote teams. The ability to leverage not only proximate but a comprehensive network of remotely-located competencies and resources in the development, production, and distribution of products and services is an enormous competitive advantage for those who can master it.

About Katie Gove

Katie Gove has more than 20 years experience in strategy, innovation, and change primarily focused on innovative partnering, outsourcing, knowledge management, and creative networks. Katie is based in Denmark and works internationally, primarily in Europe and North America. Her industry experience ranges from consumer products to pharmaceuticals to technology. Katie is Managing Director at Trellis. Trellis delivers strategic and operational services that help its clients to achieve better outcomes in outsourcing and partnering. Clients are typically engaged in knowledge-intensive outsourcing, i.e. outsourcing to build and/or deliver products and/or services. As such, most clients come from product development or R&D organizations.

Use Your Remote Teams Right - Industry Secrets From an Insider

By: Nataly Veremeeva

Lessons Learned in Managing Offshore and Nearshore Teams

(A vendor's point of view)

Outsourcing, remote teams, cost saving, and globalization are the modern phenomena we are all involved in. If hardware can be made in China and other cost-saving regions, then it is almost a crime not to do it with software – these goods do not need to be taken anywhere by train, go through customs procedures, or incur transportation risks. Internet, secure channels, code repositories, e-mails, Skype calls – and voila, you have a remote team working for you.

I take for granted that you've already made up your mind about why you need a remote team. Access to great minds of the world, lower costs because of lower salaries in the chosen region, the ability to quickly scale up to meet the challenges of your business – these are only a few possible reasons. You name yours. But once you have decided you want to go there, you face your next challenge – how not to screw up the whole thing. I have chosen, from my point of view, three most important problems that might appear when setting up remote teams, and have described the ways to avoid them.

1. Make Sure You Have Clear Goals and Good Project Management

The worst thing you can do with your project is to hope that you will give it to some company and a miracle will happen; with no effort on your part, your project quickly becomes very popular, bringing you money and visitors.

Well, I have to disappoint you here; if you do not have clear goals about why you want to work with a remote team and what exactly you need to do, nobody can set them for you. This is the key business aspect – know where you are heading, what you plan to achieve, how you get there, and what resources you need to achieve your goal.

Some companies set out for free sailing with only a dim understanding about their goals. Such projects can become a complete mess, especially when the partner company also does not have a proactive attitude.

In the beginning of my career I had one project that taught me a lot. The project needed one person full time and was supposed to be managed by the American client. We agreed to these requirements and assigned a mid-level developer.

The first task was to change the names of table fields and variables. I can imagine hairs rising on the heads of readers with a technical background. "Why?", you would ask. They were not quite sure what they wanted to do, they wanted to keep us busy, and they did not like the naming style of previous developers. So they had this great idea of the first task. We were silly enough to start doing it. And... you can imagine the mess we had in the end. We were not able to create a working version of the project and all the code was messed up. We had to rollback the changes and finally persuaded our client to cancel the task.

That was not the only problem we faced. We did a bit more work on the project, but again we did not succeed. One of the next tasks was to add a button to the system. And our client honestly did not understand that adding a button was not only a graphic manipulation but also additional code, and that the volume of work is counted not in a couple of hours, but in days and weeks. We evidently lacked good project management and technical competence from our client's side. The company I worked for was also not very experienced then, so neither they handled this situation right, nor did our client. The result – the project was stopped and closed. This project taught me a lot, and now before starting any collaboration, I make sure that we have everything settled and properly organized.

So, before sailing into the open sea of collaboration, it is very important that:

- **You clearly understand what you want to get.**

    Set your goals and define exact tasks that help in reaching the goals.

- **You deliver your goals to the chosen company.**

    Calls and meetings are the best ways to do that. Speak to the management and to your future team, give them the company presentation, tell them about your business objectives, and what you expect from them. Look for feedback, check their emotional attitude towards what you say and show, and make sure that they have understood your idea.

- **You make sure that the company has all the required information.**

    Gather all available documentation on the project, send it and, ideally, support it with an oral explanation via a team conference call.

- **You set the effective processes, using all technical advances.**

    Make sure that you do not reinvent the wheel and use the required systems, like code repository, project management system, bug tracking system, messengers, and whatever else is needed for your project.

- **You clearly define who is going to manage the project.**

    It is hard to overestimate this aspect. Proper management is one of the critical parts; it determines if your project is a success or a failure. Whether you decide to assign a person from your company or from the executor company to manage the project, make sure that, in both these cases, he or she has the required knowledge and capabilities to do that. The best case is to have responsible people from both sides, who will together manage the project and resources from the respective sides. In any case, the roles and responsibilities must be carefully detailed. Usually, proper work organization is also a matter of creativity, as you need to build a smooth process and define levels of control with a certain level of freedom that is essential for a really productive environment. The scheme I most commonly see succeeding is the following:

- You have a project manager from your side who is responsible for managing the remote team.

This person delivers the general vision for the project, assigns high-level tasks, and controls the execution.

- Your vendor company assigns a project manager or team lead or at least a senior developer with management skills from their side. This is your technical point of contact from the remote team.

This person reports to your project manager, and also has the right to participate in discussions and give opinions. He or she gets the high-level tasks from your project manager, divides them into subtasks, creates a roadmap and project plan, discusses technical details with your project manager, agrees on task volumes, and distributes these subtasks among the remote team members, using his knowledge of the skills of each developer and choosing the best suited executor for each task.

- You have a fixed account manager for your project.

With the account manager, you can discuss organizational topics, share concerns about the work of the team, and discuss ways to solve problems or increase motivation.

By setting your goals and having well-thought out project management in place, it will be much easier for you to reach your goals, make your project a success, and enjoy the benefits of your efforts.

2. Make Sure You Establish Good Emotional Interaction With People

It is hard to overestimate this point. Poor communication and poor mutual understanding result in developers starting to treat clients as money bags. The work becomes mostly compulsory, with robots doing only and exactly what you tell them to. Moreover, clients start to suspect that developers are not very smart, become dissatisfied, and in most cases, either end the project or change the strategy.

Motivation works not only inside the company, but also with remote teams. Yes, you outsourced work but you still work with people, not machines. These people also want to be part of something significant, so give them this possibility. People need some big idea for which they will work. They need to get excited and see the big picture they are working towards. So tell them about your plans and business ideas.

Another related point here – lack of interaction between in-house and remote teams. Your teams need to work well together, otherwise lack of communication will result in poorly coded parts of your software, problems with integration of different modules, problems with speed of development, and many more.

So, make sure that your people on both sides work well together. If you invest time and effort in creating the feeling of one team, they will start working together for your benefit.

In my previous job, I had a wonderful example of how a skillful director of a promising startup made this whole thing work, and enjoyed success in the end. He requested us to set up a remote team for him. We started with setting up a small team of 4 people – 3 developers and a project manager. The project manager on our side was a very clever person, but with a pessimistic view on life. Due to this, the whole team initially felt negative towards the client. They did not know him as a person. The whole idea of the startup looked crazy so, they worked mostly because the client paid; they did what he requested, but they did not believe in the success of the project.

The situation changed dramatically when the company owner first came to see the team. Fortunately, he already had experience in managing teams and knew what he wanted to get and how to get there. So he came and spent a week with the team. He made a presentation of the company and his ideas, explained how he planned to achieve his goals, how the team could help him get there, and the advantages that would bring to them. At the end of each day, we had dinners in cafes, pubs, and restaurants, during which the team communicated with their client informally. We even went to nightclubs several times and our client showed miracles of self-organization, partying till 5, and then having the usual team meeting at 9 a.m.

After this visit (which was not the only one), the team started to respect their client and felt they added value to this project. The atmosphere changed. Add to that, daily calls with quick reports on who is doing what, visits of the guys from the remote team to the client's premises, and you will understand that the whole enterprise became successful.

The problem with communication was totally solved, the remote team was happy and proud to work on the project; they respected their client and the collaboration within the team became healthier. The result – now it is no longer a startup but a steady successful company with good and constantly developing products. The team of developers in Ukraine still works on this product and though they had to solve a number of problems as they progressed, they were successful and solid in the end.

Therefore, in order to create good cooperation between your in-house and remote parts of the team, you need to do the following:

- **Visit your team and deliver the goal, mission, and values of your company.**

    Provide a general idea of the project they are working on. Stay a couple more days after you do that just to communicate informally.

- **Party with your team.**

    Create opportunities for informal team-building activities like barbeques or dancing in a nightclub or singing with a guitar after a couple of Friday beers.

- **Invite your team to work at your premises.**

    Let your in-house and remote teams solve some common tasks. Do not forget about parties.

- **Speak with the entire team on a daily basis.**

    Even if it's a 15-minute morning stand-up call, practice it on a daily basis. Let your team share plans and problems they faced. You will see that the problems will be solved quicker and plans have more chances of being realized when they are thought of and explicitly formulated aloud. Besides, everyone will know who is doing what and, therefore, will know whom to address; this also increases the overall team efficiency.

The saying that people are your strength is valid not only for in-house developers. If you treat your remote team with the same degree of attention, you will see a big difference in the results. Invest your effort in this and enjoy the benefits.

3. Micromanagement: Don't Try to Control Everything and Listen to the Advice of Your Remote Team Partner

The company is here, you are there. Take time and effort to choose the right company, visit it, and get acquainted with the CEO and those who will work on your project. Choose creative and responsible teams. After the selection, trust your partner. Do not try to control everything. In their sphere of operation, your partner company often has more information for a well-grounded decision than you. Everyone should specialize in what they are best at. If you hired this team for a specific service, listen to ideas of your partner and consider their advice about the resources and team management nuances. Otherwise, you will do more harm with your micromanagement, than getting any benefits.

In my last assignment, we had a project in which one client company wanted to get a dedicated person to solve their tasks. They initially wanted two people. We sent them the CVs and they chose one developer. But we as insiders knew that this developer will work well only when coupled with the other developer who was stronger in organizational aspects and was actually quite good as a project manager. We persuaded the client to give us the power to set the tasks on the project to the best of our knowledge. We agreed to work by calculating hours. Although the number of hours was equal to one person working full time, in reality, 3 guys worked part time, each with his own skills. Result – we finished all the tasks on time, on budget, and with the highest quality. We were lucky that the client was wise enough to listen and follow our advice and used our development possibilities to the fullest.

So, if you have made a good choice and have chosen a professional proactive team, do not overrule, but welcome the collaboration. The project, in general, will only benefit from such a synergy.

What you can do to avoid micromanagement aspects:

- **Give a general task.**

    Clearly communicate what you want to achieve, but do not go into minor technical details. Just set the problem, share your ideas, and listen to the feedback of your team. Formulate a high-level task and important criteria for its successful realization.

- **Delegate the planning and responsibility for minor aspects.**

    On the vendor's side you should have a project manager or an experienced team lead, who analyzes the task, divides it into subtasks, and gives it to a person with the best skills for that subtask.

- **Control the execution of the task as a whole.**

    Do not control each executor of subtasks separately. Instead, let your project manager on the vendor's side be the person responsible for the proper execution of the task and allow this person to control the realization of the subtasks. Delegate responsibilities. Since you do not go into details, the team has more space to choose the optimal way and feel more responsible for their actions.

- **Control the budget and timing.**

    Again, when the task is discussed and planned, ask your remote project manager to lay out the roadmap and to divide your task into subtasks and estimate them. Discuss the technical aspects, listen to suggestions from your team, correct these if needed, but let them also share their ideas and discuss their viewpoints. It is possible that they will offer you a better way to solve problems than the one you have thought of. If not, you will never lose anything if you spend some time sharing ideas. Psychologically the team will also feel involved in the thought process, and, hence, will take more responsibility for the project development.

    At the end of this brainstorming, when everything is clarified, ask the team to create a plan and estimate the hours needed to complete the task. After the planning and volume of work are formalized, control their execution.

I understand the huge temptation to control even the minor details of the work. On the other hand, delegating and sharing responsibility allows you to focus on much more important tasks which are critical for overall success like defining and sticking to business objectives, preparing sales and marketing side, onsite team management, etc.

So, these are the descriptions of three most common mistakes and ways to avoid them. Please note that each project still requires its special approach. So, use the advice reasonably. In some cases, micromanagement will be required, whereas for others, daily team meetings will be redundant. Analyze the situation and choose the right tool for each case. However, I hope these advice and real-life examples will help you avoid common mistakes and build a solid working relationship with your remote team.

Good luck!

About Nataly Veremeeva

Nataly Veremeeva – an active individual with passion for IT and making the world a better, closer, and friendlier place. Her degrees and experiences cover international management as well as language and culture. IT outsourcing with its mix of cultures, management challenges, and practically infinite possibilities for international collaboration excites and inspires her. Having worked in IT outsourcing for more than 7 years (since 2005), Nataly knows the risks, problems, advantages, strengths, and weaknesses of outsourcing, and what it takes to make it a success. And she is happy to share them.

About Intercomputer Global Services

Intercomputer GS is a European software development team provider and system integrator with development offices in Germany and Ukraine. Intercomputer GS operates in:

- **Document Management Systems and Solutions**

    Working with big enterprises and SMEs, implementing ECM systems such as Documentum, SharePoint, Alfresco, and others mostly for enterprises from financial sector and industries.

- **ODC Centers**

    Creating software development teams on a range of technologies, such as SharePoint, Documentum, .NET, Java, C/C++, and embedded development mostly for software companies that wish to extend their capabilities and increase their competitiveness in a challenging market such as IT.

- **QA Lab**

    Testing our own and our clients' products to increase quality and profit.

Intercomputer enjoys an excellent reputation since its start in 1999. It is a partner of EMC, Microsoft, ABBYY, Oracle, VMware, IBM, and Intel. It is ISO certified and has established good processes. The company has European and US clients on a wide range of services, providing them with European quality and Eastern European prices.

The Art of Managing Remote Teams

"We hope you had a pleasant reading and now have some new and useful knowledge that will help you in your work and bring you success!

In the near future the next eBook in this series of eBooks on "The Art of Managing Remote Teams" will be published! This second book will guide you through the preparations for offshoring.

To get the latest news and updates about the release, please go on to our website and fill in your details: http://bookoffshoring.bridge-outsourcing.com/

To get in contact with us, just send an email to h.messer@bridge-outsourcing.nl